# Blockly

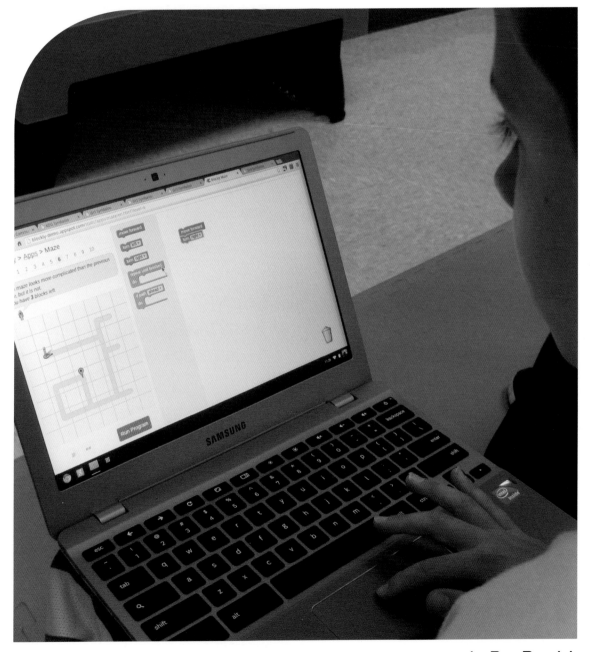

CHERRY LAKE PUBLISHING • ANN ARBOR, MICHIGAN

by Ben Rearick

A Note to Adults: Please review the instructions for the activities in this book before allowing children to do them. Be sure to help them with any activities you do not think they can safely complete on their own.

A Note to Kids: Be sure to ask an adult for help with these activities when you need it. Always put your safety first!

Published in the United States of America by Cherry Lake Publishing
Ann Arbor, Michigan
www.cherrylakepublishing.com

Series Adviser: Kristin Fontichiaro
Photo Credits: Cover and pages 1, 8, and 26, Kevin Jarrett / tinyurl.com/
jau4l3o / CC BY 2.0; page 4, Iwan Gabovitch / tinyurl.com/h76gy3t / CC BY 2.0; pages 7, 9, 10, 11, 12, 13, 15, 21, 22,
27, and 29, Ben Rearick; page 17, Carlos Luna / tinyurl.com/hoo64t7 / CC BY 2.0; page 18, Official GDC / tinyurl.com/
jslu5ua / CC BY 2.0; page 19, Curt Smith / tinyurl.com/j5u7uyj; CC BY 2.0; page 23, Jay Inslee / tinyurl.com/zg875qv /
CC BY-ND 2.0; page 24, San Jose Library / tinyurl.com/hjbgn6j / CC BY-SA 2.0

Library of Congress Cataloging-in-Publication Data has been filed and is available at catalog.loc.gov

Cherry Lake Publishing would like to acknowledge the work of the Partnership for
21st Century Learning. Please visit www.p21.org for more information.

Printed in the United States of America
Corporate Graphics

**21st** Century Skills INNOVATION LIBRARY

# Contents

## Chapter 1

# Welcome to Blockly

**Y**ou might think your computer is pretty smart. After all, it can do all kinds of incredible things. However, a computer does only what a person tells it to do. It can only do such amazing things thanks to the work of smart, creative computer programmers. In the past, programmers had to learn their jobs the hard way. They wrote line after line of **code** and told

What's going on here? These words aren't nonsense. They're computer code.

When you tell a computer what to do, you have to be very specific. If you want a computer to draw a circle, you have to tell it how big to make the circle and what color it should be. You might also need to tell the computer how quickly to draw the circle and how many circles to draw before stopping. If you're not careful, a computer could go on doing something forever in a never-ending loop!

computers how to do things like solve math problems. Today, there's a more fun way to learn about computer programming. Using Blockly, even beginners can create their own computer games and other cool programs.

Blockly is a language you can use to communicate with a computer and tell it what to do. Different languages are used to communicate with different people and things. Languages can be written down or spoken aloud. They can even use hand movements or be drawn with pictures. Languages used to communicate with computers are called programming languages. Most programming languages use a combination of words, numbers, and symbols. They can be very complex and tough for beginners to learn. Blockly uses blocks shaped like puzzle pieces.

## Types of Blocks

The blocks in Blockly are divided into groups based on the thing they can do. These groups are organized by colors.

- *Purple* action blocks tell the character on the screen what to do. This can be turning, moving, or any other action. You can make a character carry out one action after another by stacking purple blocks together.

- *Green* blocks are loops. They tell characters to do an action over and over until something specific happens. You place other blocks inside the green blocks.

- *Blue* blocks tell a character to check to see if something is true. The character can then complete different actions depending on the situation. For instance: *Is there a path to the right? If yes, turn right. If no, keep moving straight.*

Most blocks have little drop-down menus so you can adjust the details of how they work. Simply click on the arrow on a block to change the amount or style of what you want to do.

To move a connected group of blocks, just select the highest block. All of the blocks underneath will stay connected. If you want to remove a block, select it and move it to the side or back to where you selected it from.

You can simply combine these blocks into a list of instructions for a computer.

When you create a computer program, you have to follow rules just like you do when forming sentences in English. There are many rules to follow when using English. Following these rules when speaking

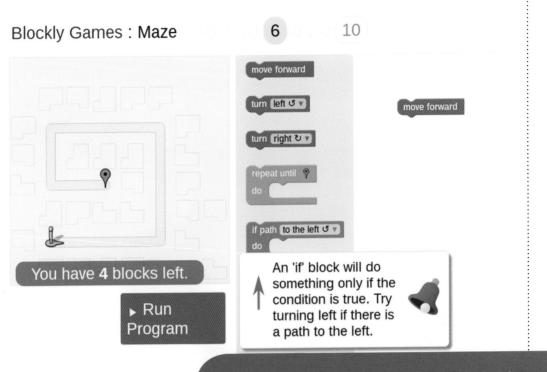

Blockly gives you a lot of hints to help you learn. On the left side of the screen, Blockly tells you how many more blocks it would take to complete your code. The pop-up box with the bell reminds you what a certain block will do.

or writing makes it easier for people to make sense of what you are saying. But if you make a small mistake, people will probably still be able to understand what you meant. This isn't true for computers. If you make a mistake when writing code, the computer will not know what to do. This could lead to your program working incorrectly or not working at all.

Because traditional programming languages are so complex, it can be easy to make small mistakes.

Students everywhere are learning the basics of computer programming through Blockly.

By using blocks instead of normal computer code, Blockly makes it easier to avoid mistakes. The instructions you create using Blockly will always make sense to your computer. However, they might not always do exactly what you expected!

Blockly was invented as a way to get young people started with coding much earlier than they used to. For many years, programmers didn't start learning to code until high school or later. But Blockly makes it easy for elementary and middle school students to get a head start in learning how to program computers.

Chapter 2

# How to Learn Blockly

lockly was created by Google as a way to help simplify the idea of coding. This way, more people could learn code quicker and create more things. Even though Blockly is simpler than traditional programming languages, there are still a few things to learn before you get started. Google created a few simple games to introduce people to the

Try Blockly

The Blockly library adds an editor to your app that represents coding concepts as interlocking blocks. It outputs syntactically correct code in the language of your choice. Custom blocks may be created to connect to your own application.

LEARN MORE

Built with Blockly

Blockly is being used by hundreds of projects, most of them educational:

When you visit the Blockly home page (*https://developers.google.com/blockly*), this is the first thing you will see.

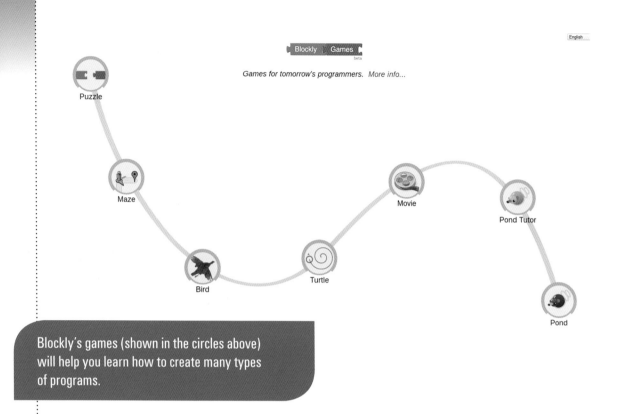

Blockly's games (shown in the circles above) will help you learn how to create many types of programs.

different ways you can use Blockly. These games will teach you the basics of coding with Blockly, step by step. You can play all of them online at *http://blockly-games.appspot.com.*

## Puzzle: Introducing the Blocks

In the first game, you will learn how different blocks fit together in Blockly. Instead of the regular Blockly pieces, you will use blocks showing animals and their various traits. Each block can either connect above,

Blockly Games : Puzzle

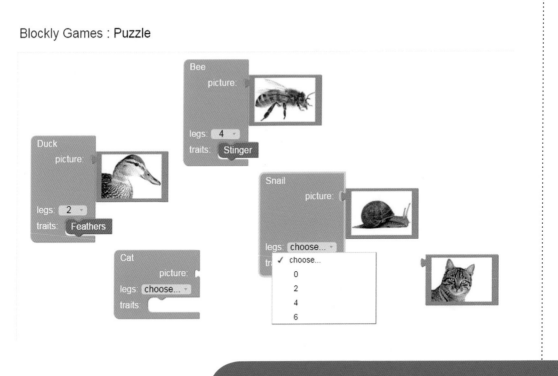

Blockly's Puzzle game is a great way to see how different blocks fit together. How many legs does a snail have? Zero! (They have a foot but no leg!)

below, or inside another piece. The descriptions of animal traits and pictures will help you see where the different blocks belong. While this game is simple, it is important to understand the basic method of putting pieces together.

## Maze: Introducing Loops

In the next game, you use blocks to program a path for a character in a maze. If you make the character go off

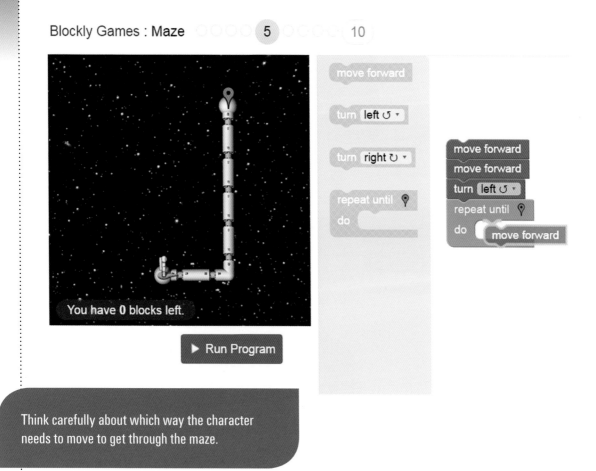

Think carefully about which way the character needs to move to get through the maze.

the route, it will fall off. Don't worry, though. You can just restart the level by clicking Reset. (If the character seems to be taking a long time to do things, you can click Reset at any time!) The mazes get more complicated as they go. They will teach you how to place blocks in the correct order so your program works correctly.

## Bird: Looking Closely at Conditions

The next game involves a bird that needs to pick up worms and reach its nest. Unlike the Maze game, there is no certain path to take. You'll tell the bird not how many blocks to move but in which direction, using degrees. (Click on the purple "heading" block and a compass will pop up to help.) It is also helpful to pay attention to the x-axis (along the bottom of the screen)

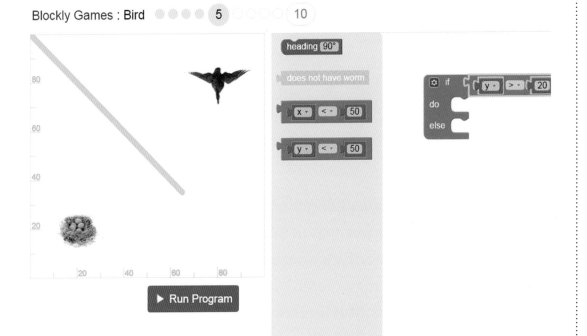

The Bird game is a little tougher than the previous ones. You need to think about direction to solve it.

## What Makes Blockly Different?

Blockly's creator, Neil Fraser, created his programming language to be "inviting, appealing, unlimited, and relevant." All of these things are very important for getting students interested in programming. This is why Blockly is a perfect fit for schools and anyone who is new to programming.

Blockly works right in a web **browser**. This means anyone with a computer and an Internet connection can use it. "Blockly is free, has no downloads, no plug-ins, and no installation. It is literally a click away," Fraser wrote after Blockly was released. This is what he means by "inviting" and "appealing."

When Fraser calls Blockly "unlimited" and "relevant," he is referring to the way it allows users to easily move on to more complex programming methods. Once you know how to use Blockly, you can transition to typing code out by hand.

and y-axis (along the left side of the screen) to figure out your position in this game. This will teach you how to use Blockly's blue condition blocks.

### Turtle & Movie: Drawing Things with Loops and Math

Turtle is a game that teaches you how to draw things with a cursor that moves and draws in the direction you tell it to go. This game is a lot tougher than the earlier ones, so be sure to understand everything in the other games before starting.

Like Turtle, Movie asks you to move an object on the screen. This time the objects are a little bigger. This game also introduces a time limit during which the objects will move across the screen.

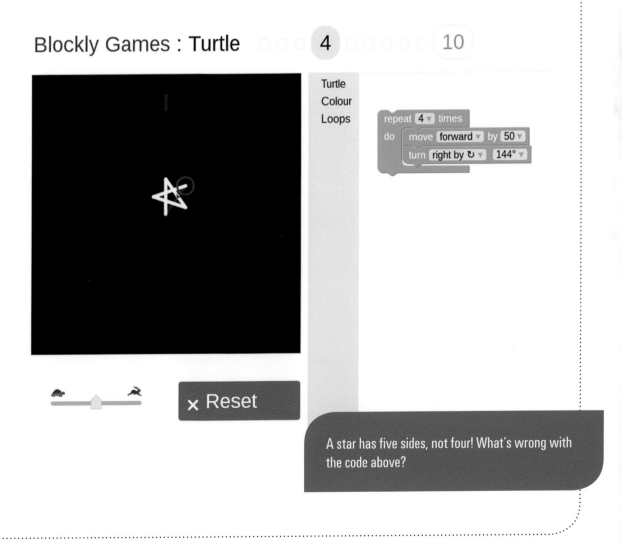

A star has five sides, not four! What's wrong with the code above?

### Pond: Using Blocks and Typing Code

The final game in the set is about toy ducks fighting in a pond. You will need all the skills you learned in the first five games to be successful in the Pond game.

If you can complete each of these games, you will have a very good handle on the basics of Blockly. Don't worry if you don't win these games on the first try, though. It might take some practice. **Debugging**, or finding and fixing problems in your code, is an important part of any coding project. You are free to make mistakes because it's just a game! If you get stuck on certain games, try thinking your program through step-by-step. Reading through the directions on each level can also be very helpful. Remember, the computer will do exactly what you tell it to, so pay attention to the details.

Chapter 3

# The Founder of Blockly

**H**ave you ever been so excited about something that you spent all your free time working on it? Neil Fraser started writing the code for Blockly during a vacation from his job at Google. He worked so hard that when he presented the finished project to Google, his boss gave him back his vacation time!

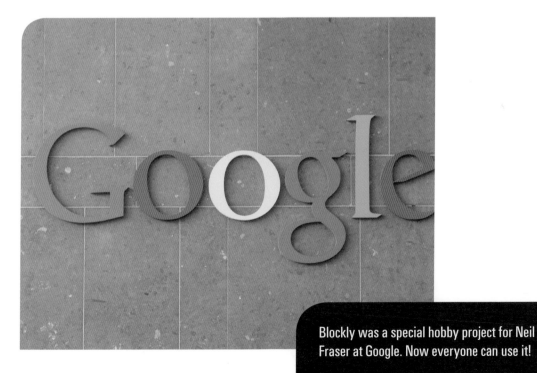

Blockly was a special hobby project for Neil Fraser at Google. Now everyone can use it!

Developers work together to create programs and solve problems.

When you really believe in something, it's easy to work hard.

Fraser isn't the only person who worked on the Blockly project. When you make such a big program, you need a team of **developers**. Sometimes a single person like Fraser might take the lead and do a lot of work. Other times team members break into smaller groups to work on specific parts of the project. Think of it as being like putting together a jigsaw puzzle with your family or friends. One of you will focus

As with a puzzle, it can take many programmers to finish a job.

on the corners, while another focuses on a group of pieces that all have the same color. At the end, you will all have a completed puzzle to admire and show to others!

Fraser's team did a surprising thing after they finished creating Blockly: They released the entire code for the program for free! This means that other developers can use their work to create their own versions

## Open Source

When a computer program is called "open source," this means it is freely available on the Internet. Other people can take all or part of the program's code and use it to make other programs. In return, these people must make their creations open source, too. They must also credit the creator they borrowed code from. Open source programs support the idea that people can create amazing things by sharing their work and ideas with each other.

Collaboration is extremely important to Blockly and other open source projects. Blockly's creators want to help teach people around the world, and Blockly has already been translated into more than 40 languages. This means if you create something new with Blockly, you can easily share it with everyone else on the Internet!

of Blockly. But why would Fraser and his team work so hard on something only to give it away?

Blockly's main purpose is to introduce more people to computer programming. By making it free for everyone to use, its creators have ensured that as many people as possible will get the chance to learn about programming.

## Chapter 4

# Code.org and Blockly

n 2013, brothers Hadi and Ali Partovi started an organization called Code.org to help encourage computer programming education for elementary, middle, and high school students. The Code.org Web site is home to a wide range of resources for students and teachers to learn more about programming.

**20,903,986,642 LINES OF CODE**
**WRITTEN BY 14 MILLION STUDENTS**

Code Studio is home to online courses created by Code.org

20 hour courses for
## Computer Science Fundamentals (all ages)

### Course 1
Start with Course 1 for early readers.

Ages 4-6

### Course 2
Start with Course 2 for students who can read.

Ages 6+ (reading required)

### Course 3
Course 3 is a follow-up to Course 2.

Ages 8-18

### Course 4
Students taking Course 4 should have already taken Courses 2 and 3.

Ages 9-18

### Accelerated Course
Learn basic computer science in an

### Unplugged Lessons
If you don't have a

Code.org is a great place to learn more about Blockly and other programming languages.

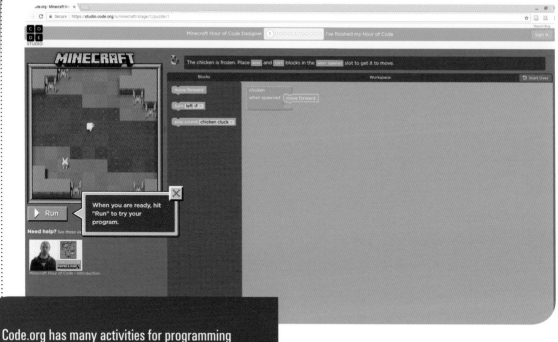

Code.org has many activities for programming students of all skill levels.

Many of its projects and activities were built using Blockly. These are a little different from the standard version of Blockly you might be used to seeing. Some of Code.org's Blockly activities use characters from *Minecraft* and Disney movies to help you learn how to code. Code.org even has games for teaching coding to students who haven't learned how to read yet. From pre-reading to high school, Code.org has enough games to keep you busy learning for a very long time!

In the past, girls and minorities were not often encouraged to become computer programmers.

Students of all ages use Code.org to study programming.

Code.org is working actively to change this. They believe that everyone, no matter their background, should have the chance to learn programming skills. Additionally, Code.org is working to create laws in the United States to make sure programming and other computer skills are taught from kindergarten all the way through high school.

Code.org hosts an annual event called Hour of Code that takes students through an hour-long

Students participate in an Hour of Code event in 2014.

**tutorial** using fun games and the world's most famous computer celebrities. Mark Zuckerberg, the founder of Facebook, has given a short tutorial on the basics of using loops with Blockly. Even Bill Gates, the

**Blockly at the White House**

On December 8, 2014, President Barack Obama invited students who had been using Code.org and Blockly to visit the White House. President Obama wanted to encourage girls and minorities to continue coding throughout their entire education. He also became the first president of the United States to write a computer program. He used Blockly!

world-famous founder of Microsoft, has donated his time to Code.org with a short video about using Blockly.

Chapter 5

# What Can You Do with Blockly?

**F**or the most part, Blockly is all fun and games. But as you master more and more of the games, you might want to try some harder challenges.

Have you ever had an idea for improving *Minecraft*? You can make your idea a reality with Blockly!

Creating *Minecraft* mods is as easy as snapping Blockly pieces together.

Blockly has been combined with other programs, games, and toys in many creative ways.

*Minecraft* is a well-known video game played by millions of people around the world. But did you know that you can use Blockly to create **mods** to make the game even better? You can change the appearance of characters, alter the way items work in the game, and

## Go Beyond Blockly!

Once you have mastered Blockly, you can start writing code without blocks! This is how professional programmers do their work. Many of the more advanced Blockly games you find online will help you make the switch from using blocks to typing out your own code by hand. With these skills, you'll be able to start learning the same programming languages that pros use to build your favorite video games, apps, and other **software**. Some popular programming languages that Blockly can prepare you for include JavaScript, Python, and PHP.

much more. You can even build your own **servers** for other players of *Minecraft* to join. If you have a good grasp of Blockly, you can quickly learn how to make *Minecraft* characters and worlds that do almost anything you want them to!

You can also use Blockly to program robots and make them do all kinds of interesting things. For example, Dash and Dot (*www.makewonder.com*) are a pair of rolling robots that can be programmed using Blockly to complete a variety of creative tasks. You can create programs that make these robots dance, play games, and much more.

There is no limit to the amazing things you can do once you learn how to write code and program

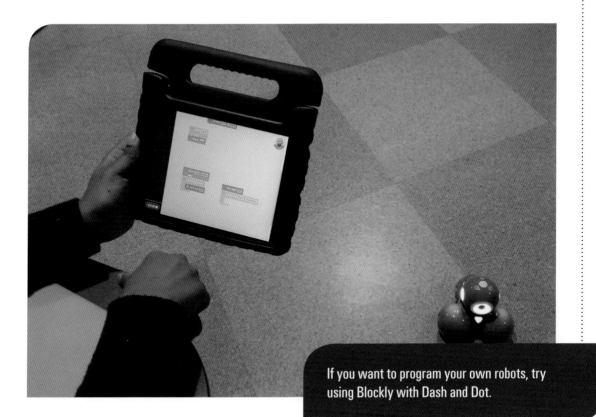

If you want to program your own robots, try using Blockly with Dash and Dot.

computers. If this sounds fun to you, Blockly is a great place to learn everything you need to know. So what are you waiting for? Go online and get started with coding!

# Glossary

**browser** (BROW-zur) a program used to access the Internet

**code** (KODE) the instructions of a computer program, written in a programming language

**debugging** (dee-BUHG-ing) searching for and removing errors in computer code

**developers** (di-VEL-uhp-urz) people who work to create computer software

**mods** (MAHDZ) programs that change the way a video game works

**servers** (SUR-vurz) computers shared by more than one user through a network connection

**software** (SAWFT-wair) computer programs

**tutorial** (too-TOR-ee-uhl) a short course in which you learn a skill

# Find Out More

## BOOKS

Benson, Pete. *Scratch*. Ann Arbor, MI: Cherry Lake Publishing, 2016.

Van Lent, Colleen. *More Web Design with HTML5*. Ann Arbor, MI: Cherry Lake Publishing, 2015.

Van Lent, Colleen. *Web Design with HTML5*. Ann Arbor, MI: Cherry Lake Publishing, 2015.

## WEB SITES

### Code.org
*https://code.org*
Check out fun Blockly activities and get other information about computer programming.

### Google: Made with Code
*www.madewithcode.com*
Check out some amazing things people have created using code.

# Index

## About the Author

Ben Rearick worked with students and teachers in Ethiopia and Sierra Leone as part of the Peace Corps. More recently, Ben studied libraries and learning technologies at the University of Michigan School of Information. He is curious about almost everything and wants to work in, on, near, or around a library one day.